ONLY THE NAMES REMAIN
VOLUME 2
Canadian, Disputed & Illinois Districts
Indian Territory - Oklahoma

by Sandi Garrett

HERITAGE BOOKS
2008

HERITAGE BOOKS
AN IMPRINT OF HERITAGE BOOKS, INC.

Books, CDs, and more—Worldwide

For our listing of thousands of titles see our website
at
www.HeritageBooks.com

Published 2008 by
HERITAGE BOOKS, INC.
Publishing Division
100 Railroad Ave. #104
Westminster, Maryland 21157

Other Books By Sandi Garrett:

Only The Names Remain
Volume 1: Flint District, Indian Territory Oklahoma
Volume 2: Canadian, Disputed & Illinois District, Indian Territory Oklahoma
Volume 3: Saline District & Cherokee Orphanage, Indian Territory Oklahoma
Volume 4: Goingsnake District, Indian Territory Oklahoma
Volume 5: Delaware District, Indian Territory Oklahoma
Volume 6: Tahlequah & Skin Bayou District, Indian Territory Oklahoma

CD-ROM - *Only The Names Remain: Volumes 1-6*

Cover illustration adapted from the illustration "Only the Names Remain"
by Cherokee artist Ralph Feather, Jr., 1995 *used by permission*

International Standard Book Number: 978-0-7884-1829-7

This book is in honor of all our ancestors that lost their home in the forced removal, also known as "The Trail of Tears."

"ONLY THE NAMES REMAIN"
CANADIAN, DISPUTED & ILLINOIS DISTRICTS
VOLUME 2

TABLE OF CONTENTS

INTRODUCTION:

I feel that linking the Drennen Roll and the Guion Miller Applications will aide many people who are trying to find their ancestors. At the time of the Drennen Roll (1851) most of the Cherokees did not have white names and many did not have last names. This only came about during the Civil War or when a census taker decided they had to have a white name.

An asterisk* beside the person in the Drennen Roll means they enrolled themselves in the Guion Miller Applications and most usually had a name change.

Whenever possible I recorded how the Guion Miller applicant was related to the Drennen Roll family. You will find the applicants name, relationship and the application number.

For example:

Family Group: #
1.   **RACHEL NEVINS**   **JOHNANAH GARLAND (GF-GGM) #881**
      JOHN NEVINS

This means Johnanah Garland was the Guion Miller (1910) Applicant #881 and his grandfather and great-grandmother are enrolled in Canadian family group #1 from the Drennen Roll (1851). Please note the name may be on the page more than once.

Abbreviations are as follows:
A.K.A. - ALSO KNOWN AS
F - FATHER
M - MOTHER
SF - STEP FATHER
SM - STEP MOTHER
S - SISTER
B - BROTHER
SS - STEP SISTER
SB - STEP BROTHER
HS - HALF SISTER
HB - HALF BROTHER
GM - GRANDMOTHER
GF - GRANDFATHER
GGM - GREAT GRANDMOTHER
GGF - GREAT GRANDFATHER
U - UNCLE
A - AUNT
GU - GREAT UNCLE
GA- GREAT AUNT

"ONLY THE NAMES REMAIN"
CANADIAN, DISPUTED & ILLINOIS DISTRICTS
VOLUME 2

Canadian District Area:

A comparison of my drawing of 1851 Canadian (Can) district, Indian Territory

The district was located in part of Muskogee (Mus) and McIntosh (McL) Counties of Oklahoma.

Illinois District Area:

A comparison of my drawing of 1851 Illinois (Il) district, Indian Territory

The Illinois district comprised the western of present Sequoyah (Seq) and Muskogee (Mus) County's

Disputed District:

This district is the most misunderstood and I think one of the most important. The land court districts did not conform to the provincial or county systems. Courts were held at different places each year in each district, so the same piece of land could be disputed in different courts at different times.

"THE DRENNEN ROLL" (1851)

The Drennen Roll (1851) lists the Cherokee Emigrants who were forced to vacate the Cherokee Nation East and the Old Settlers were the Cherokees who voluntarily moved to the Cherokee Nation West before the forced removal.

The Treaty of Aug. 8, 1846 set forth the reason for the Drennen Roll and the Old Settler Roll:
Article 9. A Fair and Just Settlement of all Moneys Due the Cherokees Under the Treaty of 1835 to be Made.

The United States agree to make a fair settlement of all moneys due to the Cherokees, and subject to the per capita division under the treaty of 29th December, 1835, which said settlement shall exhibit all money properly expended under said treaty, and shall embrace all sums paid for improvements, ferries, spoliations, removal, and subsistence, and commutation therefor, debts and claims upon the Cherokee Nation of Indians, for the additional quantity of land ceded to said nation; and the several sums provided in the several article of the treaty, to be invested as the general funds of the nation; and also all sums which may be hereafter properly allowed and paid under the provisions of the treaty of 1835. The aggregate of which said several sums shall be deducted from the sum of six-millions six hundred and forty-seven thousand and sixty-seven dollars, and the balance thus found to be due shall be paid over, per capita, in equal amounts, to all those individuals, heads of families, or their legal representatives, entitled to receive the same under the treaty of 1835 and the supplement of 1836, being all those Cherokees residing east at the date of said treaty and the supplement thereto.

Note: A roll was usually taken for disbursement of money owed to the Cherokees for one reason or another.

THE GUION MILLER APPLICATIONS

The Guion Miller Applications were taken from 1906 to 1910: Cherokee Nation East and West. There were almost 46,000 applications filed to share in the one million dollars to be distributed; the rolls used to determine who was eligible were the Hester, Chapman, Drennen and many others between 1835 and 1884. An act of Congress approved July 1, 1902 gave the Court of Claims jurisdiction over any claim arising under treaty stipulations the Cherokee tribe, or any band thereof, might have against the United States and over any claims that the United State might have against any Cherokee tribe or band. Suit for such a claim was to be instituted within two years after the act was approved. Three suits were brought against the United States concerning grievances stemming from the treaties. (1.) The Cherokee Nation v. The United States. (2.) The Eastern and Emigrant Cherokees v. The United States. (3.) The Eastern Cherokees v. The United States. On May 18, 1904, the court decided in favor of the Eastern Cherokees and instructed the Secretary of the Interior to ascertain and identify the persons entitled to participate in the distribution of more than $1 million appropriated by Congress on June 30, 1906, for use in payment of these claims. The decree also provided that the fund was to be distributed to all Eastern and Western Cherokee Indians who were alive on May 28, 1906, who could establish the fact that at the time of the treaties they were members of the Eastern Cherokees or the Cherokee Nation. The decree further provided that claimants should already have applications on file with the Commission of the Indian Affairs, or should file such applications with the special commissioner of the Court of Claims on or before Aug. 31, 1907. According to the decree, applications for minors and persons of unsound mind were to be filed by their parents or persons having their care and custody, and applications for persons who had died after May 28, 1906, were to be filed by their children or legal representatives.

"Cherokee Woman"

Cherokee woman why are you so quiet?
Have they taken your pride?
Are you giving up the fight?

Sometimes at night, I hear you cry out in vain
For all the lies that have caused you so much pain

I know you remember the trail that you walked
For all the little children that can't ever talk

The ache that you have stays in your heart
When the white man tore our Nation apart

The grief will always be in your mind
For all the people you had to leave behind

Your old life served all your needs
You didn't know of the white man's greed

What they really wanted, was all of your gold
That left all the Cherokees out in the cold

Tell all the needy
Of the broken treaties

About the forgotten braves
That now lie in their graves

The voices you hear way in the night
Are they telling you not to give up the fight?
To give back all the people's rights

Maybe they will hear that Cherokee woman who was so quiet
For she never gave up the fight, for the Cherokees rights

By,

Sandi Garrett

© 1991 CWP

"ONLY THE NAMES REMAIN"
CANADIAN, DISPUTED & ILLINOIS DISTRICTS
VOLUME 2

DRENNEN ROLL GROUP #		GUION MILLER APPLICATIONS
1.	RACHEL NEVINS JOHN NEVINS	JOHNANAH GARLAND (GF-GGM) #881
2.	JANE BUTLER	ELIZABETH SMITH (M) #11424
3.	SAMUEL BUCKSKIN LEE-SE BUCKSKIN JAMES M. BUCKSKIN	
4.	SARAH COODEY ALICE COODEY* LEWIS COODEY MARY COODEY	DANIEL COODY (M) #7997 A.K.A. ALICE WILSON #4553 WALTER SCOTT (M) #4059 DANIEL R. COODEY (F) #71
5.	ELIZABETH S. COODEY WILLIAM S. COODEY LYDIA COODEY	ELLA F. ROBINSON (M) #8704
6.	FANNY SACKETT	
7.	JOSIAH REECE	CHARLES REESE (U) #2846
8.	WILLIAM FIELDS	
9.	RICHARD FIELDS	LUCY SMITH (F) #12835 LETTIA M. WILSON (F) #4795
10.	WIRT FIELDS	LETTIA M. WILSON (U) #4795 WILLIE & LIZZIE SMITH (GF) #5666 RICHARD M. FIELDS (F) #716 RICHARD SMITH (GF) #5667 MAY FRANKLIN (GF) #5665 SAMUEL SMITH (GF) #5696 WALTER SMITH (GF) #5697
11.	WASHINGTON CAMPBELL CATHARINE CAMPBELL	JOHN CAMPBELL (SGF-GM) #14736 ISABELLE STARR (SGF-GM) #14737
12.	JOHN MONEY-CRYER	
13.	THOMAS MITCHELL JANE MITCHELL DELIA VANN* HENRY C. VANN	JOHN C. VANN (A) #3858 A.K.A. DELILAH BREWER #12726

14.	JOHN VANN	JOHN C. VANN (GF) #3858
15.	WILLIAM REECE	CHARLES REESE (F) #2846 NANCY POGUE (GF) #23283 RACHEL ROBINSON (GF) #23312
16.	DINAH	POLLY ANDREWS (M) #8346
17.	WHITE-WATER CATY WHITE-WATER	NANNIE SMITH (GF) #11863 SARAH SMITH (F) #11865 JULIETTE SMITH (GF) #17052
18.	OO-WAR-SAR-HAH	
19.	DEE-GAR-GO-WA-SKE	
20.	BENJAMIN TIMBERLEG	
21.	STAR-DEER-IN-THE-WATER	
22.	MARGARETTE OR TSE-LA-NOO-SKE	
23.	EMILY LOUISA AMANDA	
24.	WALTER SCOTT	
25.	ROBERT MATCY	
26.	SAMUEL I. RABBIT-SKIN	
27.	PEGGY MISTER	
28.	HICK SPANIARD	
29.	LUCY BOGGS	
30.	JOHN WATTS	JACOB WATTS (F) #3457
31.	CHARLES CHAMBERS MARY CHAMBERS NANCY CHAMBERS	MARTHA A. LINDER (HB) #9151
32	MARTHA VANN*	A.K.A. MARTHA A. LINDER #9151
33.	JOSEPH ORE	JAMES SEVIER (U) #11225
34.	LYDIA ORE	JAMES SEVIER (U) #11225

35.	JAMES ORE, JR. POLLY ORE ELIZABETH ORE CYNTHIA ORE AN-NIE ORE NELSON ORE	JAMES SEVIER (U) #11225 POLLY JONES (GM-GF) #3930 NANNY OER (GM-GF) #3931
36.	CATHARINE SEVIER	JAMES SEVIER (M) #11225
37.	TEE-SOR-SKEE	
38.	AGNES LEE ELIZA LEE MARTHA LEE JANE LEE LUCY LEE NELLY LEE LAURA LEE NANCY LEE	GEORGE DREW (GM) #13022 THOMAS MC DANIEL (M) #12851
39.	MARY VANN SOPHIA VANN WILLIAM VANN JOHNSON VANN	ROBERT VANN (A-U) #8756
40.	ISRAEL G. VORE SALLIE VORE EMMA VORE	MARY E. COBB (M-F-S) #2797
41.	JANE VANN JOHN VANN CATHARINE VANN JOSEPH VANN	
42.	AIL-SIE STRIKER OO-WA-STE-YOO-LAH	MARY STOP (M-F) #6483
43.	KA-HOR-KAH TE-SER-TA-SKE	
44	TEE-SIE	
45.	AIL-SIE PORUM JAMES TOM	
46.	GONE-TO-MILL	
47.	RABBIT BEAR	

"ONLY THE NAMES REMAIN"
CANADIAN, DISPUTED & ILLINOIS DISTRICTS
VOLUME 2

48.   RED BIRD

49.   KA-LA-NEE-SKE
      NEE-LAH-KA-YAH
      TSEE-YER-LOR-SKE

50.   TOO-NI-YE

51.   MISS RABBIT THIGHS

52.   MOSES OO-GUT-TE

53.   AN-NIE ROWE
      OO-TER-TA-GEE-SKE
      WUT-TE

54.   SARAH ROGERS   THOMAS ROGERS (M) #251
      TSOO-TE

55.   CU-TA-NE DOUBLE-HEAD

56.   TA-NE

57.   SUSANNAH SEVIER
      TSE-LAR-NOO-TSE

58.   BIG PATH

59.   POLLY WAR-SPEAKER
      EVA WAR-SPEAKER
      BE-HEATH-LAND

60.   CUT-TOO-CLOY
      KER-LEE-LOR-E
      QUA-TSE
      OO-SKAR-SE-TE

61.   GEORGE MORIS OR HARRIS

62.   NA-KE TUXE

63.   LYDIA JUSTICE

64.   LIZZARD BERRYHILL
      AR-LE BERRYHILL
      TAR-KE BERRYHILL
      NELLY BERRYHILL

65.	RED-HEAD A-TOR-HE	
66.	COXK PHEASANT	
67.	DAVID HUNGRY	
68.	HENRY HUNGRY	
69.	WATER MIXER	LIZZIE ETTER (GF) #8115
70.	LUCY VANN E-LE-E-SI-TE-WA-KE TER-NEE-NOR-LE	
71.	SMALL DIRT	
72.	TOO-NAR-LA-KE SAR-WAR-TSE GORDON LYDIA AUL-KIN-NE	JENNIE GIRTY (GM) #11775
73.	KAR-KE-LARW-SKE TSOO-KOR-NERN-TE DICK TER-NEE-LOR-LE NANCY WUT-TE	
74.	KER-KEM-TAH BIG KETTLE	
75.	LITTLE MEAT	
76.	JOHN BIG KETTLE*	#1716
77.	STEVEN BIG KETTLE KE-NAH-HE	JOHN BIG KETTLE (B) #1716
78.	THOMAS LITTLE-MEAT WAR-TE-YOR-HE PEGGY LITTLE-MEAT ELIZABETH LITTLEMEAT ANDREW LITTLEMEAT	
79.	QUA-TIE BIG KETTLE AUL-SE-NE BIG KETTLE	

"ONLY THE NAMES REMAIN"
CANADIAN, DISPUTED & ILLINOIS DISTRICTS
VOLUME 2

80. TAR-KE-HOG

81. WAR-LEE-YER-LIZZARD

82. MOSES HARRIS   JOHN WOODWARD (GGM-GGF) #94
    CATY HARRIS   MARTHA WOODWARD (GM-GF) #269
    ELIJAH HARRIS

83. JACK BUTCHER

84. LIGHTNING BUG

85. MIX-UP-BEANS

86. ROBERT HARRIS   MADISON CAREY (M) #2409
    HANNAH HARRIS
    NANCY HARRIS
    I-YOO-QUE-HARRIS
    OO-KER-LOR-KEH

87. WILLIAM BEAR-TOTER
    SARAH BEAR-TOTER
    TSE-YOR-SE BEAR-TOTER
    WON-NI-E

88. THOMAS STARR   KATIE GIRTY (GU-GA) #17016
    CATHARINE STARR   MARY B. JOHNSON (GM-GF-F) #10746
    LUCINDA STARR   SALLIE VANN (GM-GF) #13495
    JANE STARR   GEORGE W. CHRISTIE (A-U) #23658
    ELLIS STARR
    CHARLES STARR

89. WILLIAM STARR   GEORGE W. CHRISTIE (A-U) #23658
    NANCY STARR   KATIE GIRTY (GM-GA-GU) #17016
    MARY STARR   TOM GIRTY (M-A-U) #17017
    SUSAN STARR   SALLIE VANN (GA-GU) #13495

90. CREEK STARR   TOM GIRTY (U) #17017
    JOHN STARR   GEORGE CHRISTIE (U) #23658
    EZEKIEL STARR

91. POLLY STARR   KATIE GIRTY (GA) #17016

92. ELIZA MORE

93. RACHEL STARR   JENNIE L. CONRAD (M-F) #12837
    EZEKIEL STARR   GEORGE CHRISTIE (A-U) #23658

"ONLY THE NAMES REMAIN"
CANADIAN, DISPUTED & ILLINOIS DISTRICTS
VOLUME 2

94.	JAMES STARR	GEORGE CHRISTIE (U) #23658
95.	BLACK RABBIT	
96.	RUNABOUT	
97.	ADAM PITCHLIN	
98.	BLACK JOHN BUFFINGTON	JOHN R. BUFFINGTON (F) #3287
99.	OO-WOR-LUT-ER BUTCHER	
100.	HOXY OR NOXY	
101.	TEE-SE GUESS	SUSIE TONEY (GF) #12579
102.	MARY SHANER	
103.	BETSEY LAWRY	
104.	EDWARD BUTLER SARAH BUTLER	ELIZABETH SMITH (F) #11424 NANNY G. BUTLER (F) #2844 ROBERT MC LEMORE (M) #4596

END OF CANADIAN DISTRICT

"ONLY THE NAMES REMAIN"
CANADIAN, DISPUTED & ILLINOIS DISTRICTS
VOLUME 2

DENNEN ROLL GROUP #	GUION MILLER APPLICATIONS
1. EUNICE D. CHAMBERLAIN FLORA E. CHAMBERLAIN ALICE E. CHAMBERLAIN NELSON B. CHAMBERLAIN*	ABBIE B. TALBERT (M) #11288 ROBERT L. CHAMBERLAIN (M) #3304 LAURA CHAMBERLAIN (GF) #4272 #4276 CLARA E. CHAMBERLAIN (GM) #4273 EDWARD R. CHAMBERLAIN (GM) #4274 ARTHUR F. CHAMBERLAIN (GM) #4275
2. NANCY BALENTINE HAMILTON BALLENTINE	PERRY BALENTINE (M-GM) #11680
3. RACHEL HICKEY BEVERLY HICKEY HENRY HICKEY MARGARET HICKEY MARY HICKEY	THOMAS PRESTON HICKEY (M) #6725 NANCY MC DANIEL (M) #1489 MARY BALLARD (M) #4724 RACHEL GILMORE (F) #5580
4. NANCY ROSS*	A.K.A. NANCY MC DANIEL #1489
5. MARION POST	MARY J. MEEK (U) #3556
6. MARY HALFACRE CYNTHIA HALFACRE	ELIZA CAVALIER (M-A) #11521
7. JOHN BIBLE SUSANNAH BIBLE	BETTIE COLLIER (M-F) #15984 LETTIE THOMPSON (M-F) #15985 MARTHA DUNCAN (M-F) #15986
8. EZEKIEL MC LAUGHLIN MARY E. MC LAUGHLIN JOHN MC LAUGHLIN JANE MC LAUGHLIN DAVID MC LAUGHLIN EZEKIEL MC LAUGHLIN	EZEKIEL C. MC LAUGHLIN #787
9. LUCY NIDEFER FREEMAN* SAMUEL NIDEFER* SABINA*	GEORGE NIDIFFER (M) #8003 A.K.A. FREEMAN NIDIFFER #1814 A.K.A. SAMUEL NIDIFFER #1813 A.K.A. SABINA NIX #5843 LIZZIE MORE (B) #1745 LUCY SWAGERTY (M) #9221 EMINA J. DAVISON (GF) #1746

"ONLY THE NAMES REMAIN"
CANADIAN, DISPUTED & ILLINOIS DISTRICTS
VOLUME 2

NANCY NIDIFFER (A-C) #5682
SARAH ELIZABETH BROWN (M) #4517
RACHEL THOMASON (M) #12703
MARTHA J. WARD (M) #2145
MARY NIDIFFER (F) #22607
MAUDE NIX (M) #23128
SAMUEL NIDIFFER, JR. (F) #23133
CHARLEY NIDIFFER (F) #23463
ELLA E. MILES (F) #24496
EZEKIEL NIDIFFER (F) #24529
ISAAC NIDIFFER (F) #24550
LUCY C. SCHLICKER (F) #24840
MARY F. HIGHSMITH (F) #24975

10. MATTHEW MORE   WILLIAM MOORE (F-GM-GF) #1179
     SARAH MORE   SADIE ROWE (F-GM-GF) #15594
     DAVID MORE
     SHORTWOOD
     OO-LOO-CHA
     JOHN MORE
     KA-HAU-KA MORE
     GOO-WE-STER
     OO-DARKE-A-LER

11. ARCH BALLARD   SARAH CUNIGAN (GF) #318
                           SARAH LUCKY (GF) #5176
                           SABRINA L. MOORE (GF) #5177
                           JACKIE M. LUCKY (GF) #5178

12. JACK BALLARD   SARAH CUNIGAN (F) #318
                           SARAH LUCKY (F) #5176

13. JANE LOWREY
     ARSINOE LOWREY
     SUSAN ANN LOWREY

14. SUSAN BALLARD   SARAH A. FLINT (M) #511

15. GEORGE WARD   JOHN THORNTON (M-GF) #1119
     MALINDA WARD   SABRINA SCOTT (M-GF) #412
                           MARGARET CURRY (M-GF) #29125
                           MINNIE V. ROGERS (GF-A) #4922

16. LUCY ANN THOMPSON

"ONLY THE NAMES REMAIN"
CANADIAN, DISPUTED & ILLINOIS DISTRICTS
VOLUME 2

17. SAMUEL WARD   MINNIE V. ROGERS (F) #4922

18. NANCY STOVER

19. LUCY WARD

20. CHARLOTTE STOVER
    ELISHA STOVER
    JAMES STOVER
    LOUISA STOVER*   A.K.A. LOUISA J. HASTINGS #823
    MALINDA STOVER
    CHARLOTTE STOVER
    MARTHA STOVER
    JOHN R. STOVER

21. SABINA LARGE
    ARCHE LARGE
    ROBERT LARGE
    SARAH LARGE
    JOHN W. LARGE

22. JOHN HILDEBRAND

23. JAMES WARD

24. PATSY COUNTRYMAN
    JOHN COUNTRYMAN
    GEORGE COUNTRYMAN
    MARY ANN COUNTRYMAN
    ANDRE COUNTRYMAN*   A.K.A. ANDREW JACKSON COUNTRYMAN #579
    LUCY COUNTRYMAN
    SAMUEL COUNTRYMAN

25. NANCY CARROL   CLARINDA S. RAY (GM) #2791
    ANNA CARROL   WILLIAM T. MELTON (GM) #2158
    JANE CARROL
    CAROLINE CARROL*   A.K.A. CAROLINE FIELDS (M) #5961

26. CREASY HUMPHREYS   NANCY BLEVINS (M) #38
    WILLIAM HUMPHREYS
    JOHN HUMPHREYS*   #826

"ONLY THE NAMES REMAIN"
CANADIAN, DISPUTED & ILLINOIS DISTRICTS
VOLUME 2

27. THOMAS MUNROE

NANNIE D. HARRISON (F) #4804
CLARINDA RAY (F) #2791
SOPHRONIA HEREFORD (F) #12427
MYRTLE SANDERS (F) #14735
DORA MONROE (F) #23263
MINERVA FISK (F) #23264

28. NARCISSA MELTON
GEORGE MELTON*
NANCY MELTON
LUCY ANN MELTON
MARY MELTON*

WILLIAM CLARK (M) #2147
#2146 (M-S)
WILLIAM T. MELTON (M) #2158
ALICE SMITH (M) #2172
A.K.A. MARY DAWES #4415
MARY PARKHURST (M) #2173

29. SUSAN CARROL
HUGH CARROL

NORA MOREHOUSE (GM-F) #5495
ELLA MAY CARROLL (GM-F) #5496

30. FINCHER MONROE
JAMES MONROE

THOMAS J. MONROE (F) #6707
MUTA NEIGHBORS (F) #7946
JAMES FANNIE F. FRENCH (F) #14774
WILEY J. MELTON (F) #6708

31. SIMPSON MONROE

NARCISSUE DUNCAN (F) #1910

32. ELIZABETH FIELDS

ARCH CASEY (M) #1298
MARY M. MC CAUSLAND (GM) #11670
JOHN CASEY (M) #2184

33. MARY CLARK
EMILY CLARK*
CYNTHIA CLARK

MARY KELLY (M) #23788
A.K.A. EMILY J. BATTLES #879
BERT LYNCH (M) #23789
ANDREW LYNCH (M) #23790
EDWARD B. LYNCH (M-F) #25180
EARL C. LYNCH (M-F) #25181
RUTH WHITMORE (M) #25182

34. PEGGY NELLUMS

AGGA PHARISS (M) #279

35. SUSAN CONNER
ARMINDA CONNER
IRENA CONNER
MITCHELL CONNER
SABRA CONNER
SOPHRONIA CONNER
MARY CONNER
MARTHA CONNER

"ONLY THE NAMES REMAIN"
CANADIAN, DISPUTED & ILLINOIS DISTRICTS
VOLUME 2

36.	MARY CLARKE	KATIE J. CARMAN (M) #24063
	GEORGE CLARKE*	(M-B-S) #2919
	JAMES CLARKE	
	LUCY CLARKE	
	LOUISA CLARKE	
	JOHN R. CLARKE	
37.	NANCY RILEY	WILLIAM ROSS (M) #17632
	ELIZA J. RILEY	
38.	LYDIA HOYT	CZARINA HAMMONS (GF) #17567
	MILO HOYT	SUE HOYT (GF) #11762
		LUCY L. KEYS (M) #253
		MARY E. BALENTINE (GM) #271
39.	ESTHER HOYT	HENRY JULIAN WARD (M) #643
		DARIUS WARD (M) #3072
		CLARA WARD (M) #979
		HENRY H. WARD (GM) #23867
40.	LUCY HOYT*	A.K.A. LUCY L. KEYS #253
		MARY E. BALENTINE (M) #271
41.	HYNMAN HOYT	FLORENCE MC SPADDEN (F) #2858
42.	SARAH HOYT	
43.	DANIEL HUBBARD	THOMAS HUBBARD (F) #8152
		MOSES HUBBARD (F) #8153
		ADA STRATTON (F) #8154
44.	THOMAS HUBBARD	
45.	GEORGE PARRIS	THOMAS PARRIS (F) #23067
	MATILDA PARRIS	MOSE PARRIS (F) #23068
	MARY PARRIS	JACKSON PARRIS (F) #23070
	MOSES, JR.	LOONIE PARRIS (F) #23071
	JOHN PARRIS	CALLIE RIDGE (F) #1492
	WILKERSON PARRIS*	(M-F-B-S) #9628
	HENRY PARRIS	EDWARD PARRIS (F) #8315
	NOAH PARRIS*	(M-F-S-B) #1233
	Z. TAYLOR PARRIS	RUTHA FORBES (F) #9627
		PHENIA BEAN (F) #8317
		NOAH PARRIS, JR. (F-GM-GF-A-U) #15796
		JAMES EVANS PARRIS (F-M) #1977
		HENRY PARRIS (F-GM-GF) #2167

"ONLY THE NAMES REMAIN"
CANADIAN, DISPUTED & ILLINOIS DISTRICTS
VOLUME 2

46.	ELMIRA ROACH	SARAH SULLIVAN (M) #931
	WILLIAM ROACH	GEORGE TOWNSEND (M-A-U) #11417
	GEORGE ROACH*	#1474
	NANCY ROACH	
	JAMES ROACH	
	POLLY ANN ROACH	
	JOHNATHAN ROACH	
47.	EMILY WALLS	
	ELIZABETH WALLS	
48.	WILKERSON HUBBARD	THOMAS HUBBARD (F) #9626
	NEWTON OR WASHINGTON	ANDERSON RICHEY (GF) #1986
	JOHN HUBBARD	
49.	DAVID HENDRIX	
50.	MARY PHILLIPS	
51.	TAL-NAL H. POST	MARY J. MEEK (U) #3556
52.	MANERVA THORNTON	
53.	STOOL	
54.	MARY HARLIN	CATHERINE WASSON (M) #2111
	ELIZABETH HARLIN	
55.	JOHN HARLIN	
56.	JAMES HARLIN	
57.	JOSEPH PERDUE	JAMES S. PERDUE (F) #454
	SARAH PERDUE	
	JOHN PERDUE	
	DANIEL PERDUE	
58.	JAMES PERDUE	BETTIE WOODALL (F) #2984
59.	POLLY PERDUE	BETTIE WOODALL (A) #2984
	MARY J. PERDUE	
60.	GEORGE BEARMEAT	BETTIE WOODALL (U) #2984
61.	MARY GLADDEN	MARY J. MEEK (M-B) #3556
	WILLIAM GLADDEN	
	JOHN GLADDEN	

62.	MARY DAMMON	WILLIAM E. JOHNSON (M) #5793
	LUCY DAMMON	JESSE D. THOMPSON (M) #1230
	MARY DAMMON	WILLIAM P. PATTERSON (M) #8347
	CAROLINE DAMMON	
	MARTHA DAMMON	
63.	NO #63	
64.	GEORGE BOLING	SARAH GRITTS (U) #21141
		LUCY DUCK (F) #1931
		WOSTER BOLING (F) #10313
		CHARLES BOLING (F) #10314
		IDA B. BROW (F) #10315
		WILLIAM PEAK (GU) #4206
65.	JOHNSON BOLING	SARAH GRITTS (U) #21141
		LUCY DUCK (GF) #1931
		WOSTER BOLING (GF) #10313
		CHARLES BOLING (GF) #10314
		IDA B. BROW (GF) #10315
		WILLIAM PEAK (GU) #4206
66.	WILLIAM BOLING	SARAH GRITTS (GF) #21141
		LUCY DUCK (U) #1931
		WILLIAM PEAK (GU) #4206
67.	JESS BOLING	LUCY DUCK (U) #1931
		WILLIAM PEAK (GU) #4206
68.	CATY BOLING*	A.K.A. CATY ACORN #4631
	CHARLES BOLING	JOHN ACORN (M) #4591
		NANCY WATY (M) #4628
		LIZA ACORN (M) #4630
		DICK ACORN (M) #4633
69.	GEORGE OR WOLF	
	MULSEY	
	LUKEY	
70.	LUCY LOCKTA	
	MAHALA	
	JANE	
	SE-HO-YAH	
71.	RACHEL ROBINS	

72.	MARY QUINTON	RUTH ABERCROMBIE (M) #16735 JOEL BARNETT (GM) #3080 HANNAH DAVIS (M) #13566
73.	CATY CHOATE NANCY CHOATE DAVID CHOATE SUSAN CHOATE POLLY CHOATE	MARY MC DONAL (F-GM-A) #2857 NANCY TAYLOR (GGM) #8752 BEULAH MC CRADY (A-U) #12831
74.	CELIA FRANKLIN MARY FRANKLIN WILLIAM FRANKLIN MALINDA FRANKLIN	BEULAH MC CRADY (GM) #12831 MARY I. HOWELL (M-GM-U-A) #4037 SALLIE BRANDEWIED (GM) #5860
75.	JOHN CHOATE WILLIAM CHOATE SANDERS CHOATE JAMES CHOATE	RUFUS CHOATE (F) #62 JOHN CHOATE (F) #63 URENA COPELAND (F) #2798 CHARLOTTE FOYIL (F) #1651
76.	DELILAH HAMPTON JAMES HAMPTON SANDERS HAMPTON ISABELLA HAMPTON LOURINDA HAMPTON* SILAS HAMPTON SUSAN HAMPTON	GEORGE W. HAMPTON (M) #405 A.K.A. LOURINDA H. PETTIT #434
77.	ANNIE HYETT OR DOWNING	
78.	GOOD MONEY	BENJAMIN F. GARVIN (M) #8022
79.	WILLIAM EDWARDS	
80.	MOSES EDWARDS	
81.	JACOB BUSHYHEAD	
82.	JOHN WILLIAMS MARY WILLIAMS JAMES WILLIAMS DANIEL WILLIAMS	
83.	ARCH FOREMAN	
84.	DELILAH STARR	
85.	ANNIE JOHNSON & CHILDREN	GEORGE W. JOHNSON (F-GM) #1888

86.   MARY SMITH   HENRY HIGHTMAN (M-GM) #5386
      MARGARET SMITH   BEATRA MAYBERRY (M-GM) #5387
      MARY JANE SMITH   MAUDE BOONE (M-GM) #5388

87.   CILLY TIMBERLAKE   JONAS STILL (M) #9253
      CATY SEABOLT   SALLIE COCHRUN (GA) #11854
      RUTH SEABOLT   WILLIAM DIXON (GM) #146

88.   JOHN SEABOLT

89.   NANCY PARRIS

90.   REBECCA MORTEN
      WILLIAM MORTEN
      LOCKE MORTEN
      GEORGE MORTEN
      SALLY ANN MORTEN*   A.K.A. SALLIE BRIGHT (M-B-S) #130
      GATESEY ANN MORTEN
      BARSHEBA MORTEN

91.   CYNTHIA MORTEN   CORNELIUS WHITTINGTON (M) #3487
      THEODORE MORTEN   ROBERT MOTON (F) #17604
      HESTER MORTEN*   A.K.A. HESTER WILLIS (M) #5650
      JOEL I. MORTEN

92.   ARTILLA LANGLEY
      JOHN R. LANGLEY
      THOMAS LANGLEY
      PRICILLA LANGLEY

93.   ELIZABETH CRITTENDEN
      THOMAS CRITTENDEN
      LYDIA CRITTENDEN*   A.K.A. LYDIA HOLLAND #5234

94.   LUCINDA A. COLEMAN   JOEL BARNETT (GGM) #3080
      WILLIAM COLEMAN   LUCINDA C. CLARK (M) #13073
      AUGUSTINE COLEMAN   JOHN TULLY (M) #13460
      LEVI COLEMAN   NETTIE ELLINGTON (GM) #15874
      NEWTON COLEMAN   JAMES GIBSON (GM) #17089
      REBECCA COLEMAN   MARION GIBSON (GM) #16511
      RUTH COLEMAN*   A.KA. RUTH HADE #13309
                            WILLIAM GIBSON (GM) #16512
                            ALBERT CLARK (GM) #24963
                            JOHN CLARK (GM) #24964

95. ROBERT DOUGHERTY   ROBERT COLLINS (M) #5773
     RUTH DOUGHERTY
     CHARLOTTE DOUGHERTY

96. JOHN COLEMAN*   #13995
                                          SAMUEL COLEMAN (F) #18509

97. JANE MC CAY   EUGENE W. LOUTHER (M) #10355
     WILLIAM MC CAY   ELIZA LONG (M) #10654
     ALFRED MC CAY   JOHN S. MC CAY (F) #10607
     LUCINDA MC CAY   LEROY G. LOWTHER (M) #10608
     ELIZA MC CAY   MARY J. FOSTER (F) #12423
                                            REBECCA WEISS (F) #22762
                                             JAMES MC CAY (F) #22750
                                             WILLIAM H. MC CAY (F) #12222
                                             BEULAH DOTTS (GM) #17227
                                             MORRIS ISBELL (GM) #17228
                                             THOMAS ISBELL (GM) #17229
                                             JENNIE & OLIVE ISBELL (GM) #17230
                                             CHARLES, JESSEY, IVERA &
                                                BENJAMIN MC CAY (GF) #9180

98. MARY DOUGHERTY   ANDREW J. FIELDS (M) #5283
     ELIZA DOUGHERTY   ROBERT E. DOUGHERTY (F-GM-A-C) #3555
     VIRGIN DOUGHERTY   MARTHA GUTHRIE (M) #5307
     FLORA DOUGHERTY   RICHARD FIELDS (M) #5308
     JOHN DOUGHERTY
     JOHN DOUGHERTY, JR.
     MARY DOUGHERTY*   A.K.A. MARY ANDREWS #5281
     WILLIAM DOUGHERTY

99. ELIJAH SOUR JOHN

100. SABINA AUTHOR   SARAH LUCKY (GM-A-U) #5176
     NANCY AUTHOR   SABRINA L. MOORE (GM-A-U) #5177
     GEORGE AUTHOR   JACKIE M. LUCKY (GM-A-U) #5178
     FREEMAN AUTHOR   NANCY NIDIFFER (M-GM-A-U) #5682
     PATSEY AUTHOR

101. CHARLOTTE ARTHUR

102. SALLY AUTHOR

END OF DISPUTED DISTRICT

"ONLY THE NAMES REMAIN"
CANADIAN, DISPUTED & ILLINOIS DISTRICTS
VOLUME 2

DRENNEN ROLL
GROUP #

GUION MILLER APPLICATIONS

1. DELILA PARRIS
   RUTHY PARRIS*
   UPHEMIA PARRIS

   MARGARET HANAN (M-GM) #216
   A.K.A. RUTH MOUNTS (M) #766

2. GEORGE LOWRY

3. POLLY GEARIN
   HENRY GEARIN
   ELLIS GEARIN
   FOX GEARIN
   MARIA
   SARAH
   WILLIAM GEARIN
   PLATOFF LOWRY

   HENRY STARR (F) #10300
   ENORA TAPP (M) #10936
   MARY JANE PETTIT (M-GM) #4196
   CHARLES STARR (F) #10943
   JACQUELINE STARR (GF) #14784
   ELIZABETH DAUGERTY (GM) #15033
   PLATOFF L. MILLER (HB-HS) #22433

4. JANE COOKSON
   JOHN*
   ELIZABETH COOKSON
   JANE HILDEBRAND

   EFFIE NELSON (A) #4693
   A.K.A. JOHN COOKSON #11603
   JENNIE HANNON (GM-A-U) #1605

5. NANCY E. PETTIT
   CAROLINA

   JENNIE HANNON (A) #1605

6. ELIZABETH PATRICK
   JOHN PATRICK*
   ELIAS PATRICK
   GEORGE W. PATRICK*
   NANCY PATRICK
   PEGGY*
   POLLY PATRICK*

   ELIZA KOLPIN (M) #3916
   #4585
   MARY LUTZ (GM) #5909
   #564
   SARAH DOBSON (M) #4706
   A.K.A. MARGARET MORRIS (M) #539
   A.KA. MARY P. LYMAN (M) #209
   MOLLIE COSTEN (GF) #5240
   HENRY HEINRICKS (GM) #5390
   KATIE MC DANIEL (GM) #5515
   JANE HALL (GM) #22558
   MIKE PATRICK (M) #22559
   IDA JENKINS (F) #22599
   ALEC PATRICK (F) #22600
   LELIA WESTOVER (GM) #23485
   JOSEPHINE STEVENS (GM) #23486
   ELIZA SMITH (GM) #23487
   THOMAS WESTOVER (GM) #23588
   WILLARD WESTOVER (GM) #23596
   HARRY L. DOBSON (GM) #24124
   WALLACE DOBSON (GM) #24126

"ONLY THE NAMES REMAIN"
CANADIAN, DISPUTED & ILLINOIS DISTRICTS
VOLUME 2

7. ALEXANDER BALLARD   ARTEMIZA E. ETHRIDGE (M-F) #1596
    RACHEL BALLARD   LIZZIE SMITH (GGF-GA-GU) #17908
    DOWN BALLARD
    LUCY BALLARD
    T. BALLARD
    LIZZY BALLARD
    SUSANN BALLARD
    NANCY BALLARD*   A.K.A. NANCY PETTIT #2903

8. RACHEL MITCHEL   ADA E. & BESSIE R. FOWLER (GM) #12715
    HENRY B. MITCHEL   JOHN MITCHELL (B-S) #5109
    MITCHALL MITCHEL*   A.K.A. MICHEL H. MITCHELL #5107
    NANCY MITCHEL*   A.K.A. NANCY ALLEN #5108
    JANE MITCHEL   FANNIE WELCH (M-U-A) #8243
    REBECCA MITCHEL
    LOVICE MITCHEL

9. MINERVA ANDERSON

10. NANCY LOVETTE   LOUISA TROGLIN (F) #10949
    JAMES LOVETTE   ELVIRA LOVETT (F-GM) #4708
    DAVID LOVETTE   JOE IRVING (M) #10601
    JOHN LOVETTE
    ANNA LOVETTE
    LOUISA

11. JOSEPH HILDEBRAND   GEORGE MEEKER (GF) #11698
                                     EFFIE O. H. NELSON (F) #4693

12. DRAGGING CANOE
    HIS DAUGHTER NELLY

13. JAMES LUCULLA   LEVI KEYS (M-GF-U) #16160.5
    THOMAS
    POLLY
    SIMAN
    INMAN
    ELLICK
    WILLIAM

14. NANCY

15.   RUTH GRIGSBY   ELMIRA SCOTT (GM) #709
       MARY JANE
       LUCINDA*   A.K.A. LUCINDA MOHR #3499
       ANNIE
       MEHAYLEE*   A.K.A. MAHALA SMITH (M-S) #710
       RHODIE

16.   CA-LAU-NU-HAES-KEE
       ANNIE

17.   NANCY CLARK
       GEORGE
       JANE

18.   RAFT
       TUNY

19.   JOHNSON RAFT   SILA SUNDAY (GF) #11778
       HETTY
       JOHNSON W. RAFT
       RED RAFT

20.   GO-ROUND
       JANE

21.   JAMES MONEY CRIER
       NELLY MONEY CRIER
       LYDIA

22.   JOHN CAMPBELL OR MONEY CRIER

23.   WALK DEER HEAD
       SALLY OR I-YOR-KEE

24.   CAPTAIN BALDRIDGE   JOHN BIGBY (GGF) #17101

25.   BETSEY BLAG

26.   ALEXANDER THOMPSON

27.   BLACK FOX
       KATTY

"ONLY THE NAMES REMAIN"
CANADIAN, DISPUTED & ILLINOIS DISTRICTS
VOLUME 2

28.   YOUNG PUPPY
      ARNEWAKE
      FATICE
      SARAH PIGEON
      CUN-SCOW-EE

29.   AH-NAE-TE-NAE-KEE
      SOLDIER
      TA-CAR-TU-NER
      TUR-NE-YOS-CHE

30.   OO-NE-TE-NARN-TER OR SOLD
      ALEXANDER
      CUL-LE-LAU-HE

31.   YOUNG WOLF
      A-WAR-LE
      KAR-TAY-YER
      LIDDIE

32.   AVE

33.   WILLIAM MC DANIEL
      JOSEPH MC DANIEL
      JOHN MC DANIEL

34.   AKE MC DANIEL   EMMA & JAMES ROGERS (GGM) #13501
      DELILA JOHNSON   BULLET SAR-NE-GER-YAH (GM) #16417
      CHE-QUA-QUE
      WAR-LE-SEE
      NED
      SUSANNAH

35.   RED BIRD

36.   LIZZY KEE-KEE
      PEGGY
      E-TA-KER-SKER
      BETSEY

37.   ANNIE EDWARDS
      DELILA
      HENRY

38.   BETSEY MOSS

22

"ONLY THE NAMES REMAIN"
CANADIAN, DISPUTED & ILLINOIS DISTRICTS
VOLUME 2

39. JOHN RIDGE
     QUAR-LA-YUR-KE
     SUL-A-TEES-KE
     RAIN-WATER
     WHITE-KILLER

40. AITSEY OTTER
     TICK-TUS-KY
     JUDGE CHE-YAH
     TA-NER-TLE-LE

41. NA-KEE
     BLACK-HAWS CHECKEN

42. SUSAN CHICKEN
     NANCY
     SQUIRL
     LUEIJA OR LOUISA

43. LOUIS CHICKEN

44. WOODS ON FIRE
     BETSY
     CHEE-TAH-YER-LE-TAH
     NAKE
     THOMPSON

45. EZEKIEL
     SUSANNAH
     JESSE

46. JACK WIND
     LUCY WIND

47. DANIEL
     BETSY
     DICK
     AVE

48. JACK CHICKEN
     JOSEPH CHICKEN
     BETSEY CHICKEN
     CHARLOTTE CHICKEN

49. GEORGE SANDERS   DICK JUSTICE (GM) #12406
     JINSY SANDERS   MAGGIE FIELDS (M-GM) #11491
     NELLY*   A.KA. NELLIE LEAF (M) #12402

"ONLY THE NAMES REMAIN"
CANADIAN, DISPUTED & ILLINOIS DISTRICTS
VOLUME 2

50. WILLIAM BALDRIDGE   JOHN BIGBY (GF) #17101
    WAT MC CLURE
    ANNE BALDRIDGE

51. ROBERT BROWN
    SARAH BROWN
    WILLIAM BROWN
    PEGGY BROWN
    RICHARD BROWN
    TI-EN-NY

52. RICHARD SHOE-SOLE
    KATY DRY-FORE-HEAD

53. BOSTON WOLF
    WALTER WOLF

54. MARY POST   LUELLA BAKER (A-M-GM-U) #13992
    C. F. COBLE
    CATHARINE POST
    LUCY E. POST

55. MALDEREEN

56. SUSANNAH PATH-KILLER

57. GEORGE BUTLER

58. ANNA CRAWFORD   JACK CRAWFORD (GM) #11295
    MARY ANN CRAWFORD   CATY WOODALL (GM) #11296
    NELLY CRAWFORD

59. CRYING FOR MONEY

60. TE-SAES-KY
    A-YORSTE
    PEGGY

61. KUL-LOR-NURS-KY

62. FODDER

63. JACK

64. CHARLES   SUSIE ROGERS (M-B-S) #14062
    SARAH
    MARY

"ONLY THE NAMES REMAIN"
CANADIAN, DISPUTED & ILLINOIS DISTRICTS
VOLUME 2

65.   WOOL

66.   RIDER LIZZARD
      KA-TAU-CLER-NER*   A.K.A. NELLIE JOHNSON (F) #13488
      CHE-LAU-NUR-CHE
      CINDY CROW

67.   JUMPER LIZZARD
      YOUNG-BIRD
      JOSEPH LIZZARD

68.   TOUGH RED-BIRD

69.   NEELY MC DANIEL

70.   MARIA MC DANIEL
      NELLY

71.   BETSY SPANIARD OR SPRING-BACK
      LOUISA SPANIARD
      EMALINE SPANIARD
      NANCY SPANIARD

72.   BENJAMIN TANUR

73.   ELIZABETH MC DANIEL

74.   ALLEN RATLEY   FANNIE CUMMINS (FATHER-IN-LAW) #1963
      WALLACE RATLEY*   (F) #6736
      POLLY RATLEY   JOHN MC LAIN (M) #9790
      SALLY TAREPIN   WALLACE THORNTON (GU-C) #1962
      CHARLES SPANIARD
      WEE-CHEE-LE
      JINY EPSY

75.   CRAWLER HICKS   MATTIE ROGERS (GF) #7433
      JINNY HICKS
      SALLY HICKS

76.   JANE WILLIAMS   JESSE A. THOMAS (GM) #877
      OSCEOLA WILLIAMS   FANNIE RIDDLE (M) #6274
      FRANKLIN WILLIAMS   MARTHA LEE (F) #17529
      PUR-RE-LEE WILLIAMS

77.   POLLY DOWNING
      JAKE DOWNING

78. BETSY GO-IN
OOL-SKUN-NEE
HUNTER
OO-LU-CHEE

79. TE-CHA-LE-SA-TA-SKE
ARLEY
NELSON
CHU-WAE-LU-KEE
JAMES
NELLY

80. SUSANNAH

81. NELLY LOVETT   SAMUEL HENSLEY (GM) #17095
JOHN LOVETT   G. W. PETITT (GM) #2119
ALEX. LOVETT   LOUISA GILSTRAP(M) #14798
ELIZABETH LOVETT   HOUSTON, JIM & JOE HENSLEY (GM) #17096
ARCHIBALD LOVETT

82. TE-KA-TORS-KE
CLAY-YER-KA
TA-KE
DIRT-EATER

83. MARGARET FIELDS   THOMAS FRENCH (GM) #11745
LEANDE HILDEBRAND   DORA PENNEL (GM) #14094

84. TASSEL
ANNA TASSEL
JAMES TASSEL
JOSEPH TURNOVER
THOMPSON TURNOVER
PEGGY TURNOVER

85. OALE
A-LEE
OO-TER-LA-TANE

86. ELIZABETH WARD   FRANK PETTIE (M-B-HS) #1859
ANDREW PETTIT   JOSEPHINE ROSS (U-A) #2142
WILLIAM PETTIT   MATTIE ADAIR (F) #9378
FRANKLIN PETTIT*   #1859
AMELIA WARD   MAGGIE J. BRYAN (GF) #4496
       JOSEPH M. ROSS (GU) #4497

87. CORN-SILK   ELIZA PHILLIPS (GGM) #12569
   ELIZABETH CORN-SILK KATE FLENDYE PHILLIPS (GM) #2182
   NANCY CORN-SILK   CHARLES OSAGE (GM) #13762
   SUSAN CORN-SILK   JIM PHILLIPS (M) #11189
   MARIA CORN-SILK   NELLIE CHRISTIE PHILLIPS (GM) #12512
   RACHEL CORN-SILK
   LUCINDA CORN-SILK

88. SARAH FOREMAN   ERMINA C. VANN (M) #8755
   PEARCE FOREMAN   GEORGE FOREMAN (F) #17278
   EDWARD FOREMAN
   GEORGE FOREMAN

89. SUSAN BURGISS
   JOHN BURGISS
   CHE-AR-NAH-NAH BURGISS
   LEECH WOODWARD

90. AVE

91. NANCY CAT
   AH-KE-LAW-KEE

92. SE-WE WOODWARD
   BEAVER STAND

93. SARAH TRACKER
   AH-NA-CLE-LAW-HE
   THOMAS FIELDS
   ELIZABETH

94. SWELL

95. TAR-CHA-LUR-NUR
   RACHEL
   JANE

96. OO-TAE-LE-TAH MORRIS
   ALSEY MORRIS
   GOARD
   WILLIAM CATE

97. TE-LAR-SE-NE TIMBERLAKE

98. ARNE-BLACK-COAT

99. CHE-COO-WE
     AE-LE
     A-HOR-KA
     JOHN NICK
     EZEKIEL

100. LOUISA MC KAY   SAM T. FIELDS (GM) #9147
     JOHN MC KAY   LUGIE STARR (M-GF) #15046
                           JACK, NARCISSA, JOHN, JR. &
                           KELLAH BROWN (GM-U) #16550

101. AKE
     TAH-NE-SOCK-KE
     U-TAL-KE
     GO-IN-WATER
     ALSEY

102. BETSEY FIELDS
     MARTHA FIELDS

103. JAMES TAYLOR   C. F. TAYLOR (F-GF) #5670
     SARAH TAYLOR
     CHARLES P. TAYLOR
     JANE W. TAYLOR
     JOSEPH V. TAYLOR
     WILLIAM B. TAYLOR

104. CHIN-NAE-BY
     NAKE
     BENJAMIN
     CHE-CAW-NERN-TER
     BETSEY
     SUSANNAH
     E-YAR-NE

105. JOSEPH FOREMAN
     NANCY FOREMAN
     RACHEL FOREMAN
     RAVEN

106. SALLY SEABOLT
     CHU-NEAL-KAH SEABOLT

107. ARCHILLA PATH-KILLER
     TARNE
     PATH KILLER
     QUART-E-QUAT-SKE

"ONLY THE NAMES REMAIN"
CANADIAN, DISPUTED & ILLINOIS DISTRICTS
VOLUME 2

108. ARCH MC DANIEL

109. DARKEY   WILLIE RODGERS (F) #16182
      SUSAN   JOHN TONEY (GM) #17512
      LOVELY ROGERS
      LOUIS WHITE
      LUCY PATH KILLER

110. ELOW-EE
      JINLY ELOWEE
      CAW-HE-NE*   A.KA. LINDA CRAPO (M-F) #9260
      CHE-LAU-NUR-CHE
      BETSEY LOCUST
      BETSEY

111. LYDIA
      SAM

112. A-CHEE-TE-TEE-TOW-NE   ELLEN TEEHEE (M) #13635
      JINNY WEAVER
      JANE RATLEY
      DICK RATLEY
      SALLY WEAVER
      NANCY WEAVER
      GEORGE WEAVER

113. NE-HA-CHE DICK
      SAMPSON DICK
      JOSIAH DICK

114. SAR-WAL-A-PO-GEE   MAGGIE LEAF (F?) #7670
      MIS-LEETER SALE   RACHEL BUSTER (F?) #7662

115. HARPELLY
      RATTLING GOURD
      HE-HA-CHEE

116. COO-LARS-TE
      TE-CLA-KEE
      TA-YERS-KEE
      BETSEY

117. TAR-SKE-KE-TE-HEE   MACK NOISY (F) #17132
      CO-TA-NE-YE-NE-TAH
      OO-WA-LOO-KEE
      JAMES
      POLLY

"ONLY THE NAMES REMAIN"
CANADIAN, DISPUTED & ILLINOIS DISTRICTS
VOLUME 2

118. OO-NA-KER-CHE-TAH
POLLY
RAVEN

119. OO-KER-WE
NOO-CHOWER

120. QUA-NA-KE
MARTHA

121. WILD-CAT-YOUR-HOLEE   WILLIAM WILDCAT (F-M-S) #6696
SALLY   BEN WILDCAT (GM-GF) #14794
MOLLY   NANCY WEBBER (GM-GF) #14989
    SPADE WILDCAT (GM-GF) #14802
    COLE-SEE-NEE WILDCAT (GM-GF) #14803

122. CLOUD
CHE-CAU-NALE
WALKING STICK

123. PEGGY WILSON
NANCY WILSON

124. GEORGE WATERS   KATIE DEER-IN-THE-WATER (F-M) #10388
NANCY WATERS   JIM LEAF (GM) #16349
LIGHTENING-BUG
TOO-CHAH

125. ROBERT LOVETT   JOHN LOVETT (GM-GF) #1422
POLLY LOVETT

126. JOHN RAINCROW   SOPHIA L. CHARLEY (F-M) #3503
RACHEL RAINCROW*   #4721
ARCHILLA RAINCROW   JOE RAINCROW (S) #4722
ARCH RAINCROW   CHARLOTTE DEW (GM-GF) #6058
CHUNE-STEE-TE RAINCROW   JAMES COLLIER (GF) #13636
CAR-SEE-CORS   SARAH REDBIRD (GF-GGM-GGF) #15965
OO-TAL-KEE   SUSIE BUFFINGTON (GF) #15995
KER-YOU-CHE
SUSANNAH
I-YOR-KA

127. GEORGE W. LOVETT
MARTHA LOVETT
GEORGE BENGE
LEVI

128. SUSANNAH
      CHOW-E-YU-KA

129. SUNSHINE
      OO-LEE-CHE

130. AR-NOR-HE

131. EMERY OGDEN LINDER   MARY E. SMITH (F) #9152
      ANNA LINDER   HIRAM D. LINDER (F) #9150
      CINDERELLA LINDER*   A.K.A. CINDRILLA RANDEL (B-S) #4235
      JULIUS CAESAR LINDER   NANCY E. HICKS (B-S) #4234
                                  PREAN LINDER (GF) #18104
                                  OWEN LINDER *GF) #18105

132. JESSE SMOKER
      SE-TAR-NE
      AR-NOR-HE
      NELLY

133. DEW
      GROUND-HOG
      JOHNSON

134. TE-SAUS-QUE

135. KER-LARN-TA-QUA-NEE
      UT-SAL-E
      TARS-SKE-KE-TE-HE

136. CHU-WA-LU-KE
      CHOW-WAE-YU-KA
      OO-KIL-LA

137. TA-KE   BECK CRITTENDEN (F-GM-U-A) #6071
      SUSANNAH
      JOSEPH
      MOSES
      QUA-KE

138. AKE PRITCHET
      ELIZA KILLA-NETER
      KILLANETER

139. OO-WA-SEE
      NANCY
      NELSON

"ONLY THE NAMES REMAIN"
CANADIAN, DISPUTED & ILLINOIS DISTRICTS
VOLUME 2

140. LUCY RUSSEL
ALEX. RUSSELL
RACHEL RUSSEL
ANDERSON RUSSEL
W. T. RUSSEL*

IDA MILLER (GM) #11196
ROBERT RUSSELL (GM) #9720
CHARLES RUSSELL (F) #15596

A.K.A. WILLIAM T. RUSSELL #7450

141. JOE DICK
EMILY DICK
GEORGE DICK

142. STEPHEN
FINNEY STEPHEN
LEDDY STEPHEN
NANCY STEPHEN
HUMMING-BIRD
SIT-U-WA-KE

143. SE-NARSTER
GOBBLER
A-TAU-HE
SUSAN A-TAU-HE
SCAR-KOO-HER-SKEE
TE-CAR-NOO-COW-WAH-SKEE

144. PATH KILLER
FEATHER PATH KILLER
SARAH PATH KILLER
SALLY PATH KILLER

145. TE-KER-WA-SA-TAES-SKE

146. QUA-TE
TU-WA-YOH-LOH
CHE-NE-LUR-KE

147. WUTTY
JAKE POLL-CAT
MARIA POLL-CAT
CUN-NA-CHUR-NE

SEQUOYAH PANTHER (GF-GM) #7671

148. CORN-TASSEL
TE-CUS-KA TASSEL

149. SICK-CA-KEE
KILLER

"ONLY THE NAMES REMAIN"
CANADIAN, DISPUTED & ILLINOIS DISTRICTS
VOLUME 2

150. YEATH-CHE
      SALLY
      TOOKER
      KE-KER-WAH-LER-TE-SKE
      MAN-YOUNG
      DICK YOUNG
      NUNE-TE-TER-NER

151. CHU-STI-LER
      NICK-OO-TI-YER
      JUG
      WOLF-GOING-ALONG*   A.K.A. JAMES GOINS (M-F) #6644
      TE-CAW-WA-TEES-KEE
      PEGGY
      ARLE

152. QUA-TE
      CAR-NAE-LU-KEE

153. HAWK
      TA-CHER-KE-SA

154. CATY CHICKEN
      EVE CHICKEN

155. CAR-LE-LOW-HE

156. CHU-TA-YER-LA-TER
      AR-SEE-LOR

157. E. GEORGE
      MAKE GEORGE
      CRAWFISH
      TE-CAR-YE-SKE

158. LINNY   JAKE PETTIT (M) #8766
      SQUAT-A-LE-CHE

159. SAL-A-KEE-KEE OR TURTLE
      OO-TE-CA-WE
      CHA-AR-LE-TER
      NANCY
      CAR-YAH-NUR*   A.K.A. DICK PORTER (M-S-GF) #4205
      QUAITSY

160.	CHEE-WA-STE-TOR	COMINGDEER ROSIN (F) #16589
	OO-WO-TE-YOH-HE	SIMMER ROSIN (F) #16903
	OO-LU-CHEE	
	OUR-YU-CHA	
	YER-WE-LOR-SE	

161. CHICK-KOR-NALE
E-CHAR-KA

162. A-TON-HE
E-YAR-NE
OO-LU-CHEE

163. SUSAN
OO-TAL-KEE
CHU-LE-OR-HE

164. NANCY TWIST
OO-LA-CHE-SKE
CAR-NAR-HE

165. JINNY
OO-NOE-TE
NELLY

166. A-TARN-TOES-SKE

167 CATY
CHU-QUAL-KE
CHE-COO-WE

168. OO-TE-SA-TAH
QUATE
AR-NE-CHA-YER-CHA
LESTER*   A.K.A. LESTER MC COY (F-M) #6715
CHARLES
CHA-KER-WA-LEE-SKEE

169. SARAH TE-TAR-SKEE-SKE
NANCY TE-TAR-SKEE-SKE

"ONLY THE NAMES REMAIN"
CANADIAN, DISPUTED & ILLINOIS DISTRICTS
VOLUME 2

169 1/2 MARY BARNES* A.K.A. MARY WILLEY #4014
  ALBERT BARNES TEXANNA FIELDS (F) #715
  RACHEL BARNES MARY PECK (M) #6790
  ALEXANDER BARNES CATHERINE THOMPSON (M) #4013
  CORN BARNES ANNA W. FORTNER (M) #6929
  THERESA BARNES THOMAS TAYLOR (M) #10890
  HENRY BARNES MAGGIE THORNE (M) #12508
  SARAH ANN BARNES* A.KA. SARAH HART #4012
  MARY BARNES

170. CATHARINE HASTINGS STEPHEN MAXWELL (M) #7947
  NANCY HASTINGS

171. W'D ELVIRA FIELDS VETORIA PETTY (M) #8952
  SARAH ELIZABETH FIELDS GEORGE E. PAYNE (M) #8953
  GEORGE FIELDS* #6443
  ELIZABETH MC COY

172. MARTIN MC COY

173. WILLIAM MILLS MARY HAMMETT (U) #23467
  BETSEY MILLS KATE BACON (M-F) #12227
  NELSON MILLS CLIFFORD SHARP (GM-GF) #17105

174. SARAH MC KOY HENRY H. SANDERS (M) #9154
  MINTA MC KOY LOONEY MC COY (F-GF) #5902
  ALEX. STARR
  CAROLINE MC KOY
  EDWARD MC KOY
  CHARLES MC KOY

175. JAMES MILLS
  ANNA MILLS
  POLLY MILLS
  LEWIS MILLS
  GEORGE MILLS* #6608

176. ALSEY HOLMES JAMES HOLMES (F) #13761
  MARY HOLMES SIMON HOLMES (GF) #2700 1/2
  JAMES HOLMES
  DAVID HOLMES
  SUSAN HOLMES

177. RACHEL SPANIARD
  AVE SPANIARD
  CAR-YOU-CHA

"ONLY THE NAMES REMAIN"
CANADIAN, DISPUTED & ILLINOIS DISTRICTS
VOLUME 2

178. BETSEY SPENCER
      AMERICA SPENCER
      SUSAN
      MARY LEE

179. GEORGE WHITFIELD   CHARLOTTE PATTON (F) #9309
      SARAH WHITFIELD   JAMES TAPP (F-C) #3978
      MARTHA WHIRLWIND
      MARY WHIRLWING*   A.K.A. MARY CARTER #2222
      LUCY WHITFIELD*   A.K.A. LUCY LYNCH #2223
      URMINIA WHITFIELD
      DANIEL WHITFIELD
      JOSEPH TAPPEN

180. JOHN CRAWLER   WILLIAM HOLMES (M) #7424
      LYDIA CRAWLER   NANCY HARMON (M) #6720
      KATY CRAWLER   SALLIE THORNTON (F) #382
      ANNE CRAWLER
      POLLY CRAWLER
      QUAITY CRAWLER
      QUAITY
      NUM-TI-YAH-LER

181. JACK CANDY   GEORGE CANDY (F-GM-GF) #267
      DARKEY CANDY
      WHITE WOMAN
      CHU-LAW-QUA

182. NELLY
      QUA-TE-QUA-SKE
      THOMAS WATTS
      NANCY

183. HENRY CLAY CAR-TE-QUA-LER   POLLY CROW OR YA-HO-LA (GF) #11493
      YORK-SE   SUSIE PERDUE (GGF) #12401
      JOSEPH V. CLAY

184. JOSIAH
      CAR-NER-NUR-TES-KEE
      JINNY

185. MAN-KILLER
      ALSEY MAN KILLER
      JAMES MAN KILLER
      CHOW-E-U-KA
      NUME-TE-LUN-NER

186.   SAM OR SAWNEY   FISH LOCUT (M) #5803
       LUCY BARK
       CA-HE-TAH
       ROBIN

187.   FISK OR FAW-GETTING-OUT   NANCY STICKS (GF-M) #7020
       WHITE-WOMAN
       DICK
       KILLER-TOO
       SUSANNAH
       TE-SQA-NAR-LER
       TE-CAR-NEE-SKEE
       RACHEL DICK

188.   CAR-CHE-KER-WA-SKE

189.   WILSON
       LYDIA
       RUN-ABOUT WILSON*   (M-F) #6075
       JINNY WILSON
       JOSEPH WILSON

190.   A-TAW-HE
       A-KE
       LYDIA*   A.K.A. LYDIA WALKER #6932
       TAR-YAH-WAH
       TE-CAW-YAES-SKE
       E-CHE-COO
       NANCY

191.   JOHN
       SKI-HA-CHE

192.   TARNES
       ALSEY
       ARNE WAKE

193.   CHA. R. GOURD   POLLY HERBERGER (F) #4524

194.   LUCY THORNTON
       ELIZABETH THORNTON
       SAM BELL

195.   NAN PARTRIDGE

196.   DAVID VANN   ROBERT VANN (F) #8756
       THOMPSON

197. LUCY TAKES-TAS-KE
      SUSAN TAKES-TAS-KE
      CO-TE-CA-WE
      ELSEY

198. JAMES VANN   ROBERT VANN (U) #8756

199. DAY-LIGHT
      ANN DAY-LIGHT
      CHARLOTTE DAY-LIGHT
      TER-KER-YER DAY-LIGHT

200. WILLIAM LITTLE
      CAH-LAW-HUR-SHE
      STEAL-IT
      YOW-NUR-OO-NUR-WOR

201. POLLY RAIN-MAKER

202. MC COY   EVE COCHRAN (GM-GF) #5300
      OO-TI-AH MC COY   WILLIE ARCH (M) #14780
      LEECH MC COY   MAGGIE SIXKILLER (GM-GF) #2873
      CHE-LOW-NUR-CHE   ESTHER MC COY (GF) #13507
      OR-LI-KOR   ALEXANDER MC COY (F) #10904
      OON-STUR-LOW-KE   WAH-LEAS-CIE KINGFISHER (M) #2938
      KA-YU-KAH
      JACK MC COY
      TU-LE-STA MC COY
      THOMAS MC COY
      TI-AN-AH MC COY
      CHENALY MC COY

203. TE-KAR-NE-EES-KY
      WILLIAM

204. HEAVY
      YOUNG SQUIRREL
      AKEY SQUIRREL
      RACHEL
      GEORGE
      JOHNSON
      QUATSEY
      SUL-A-TES-KEE

205. NA-NA BALDRIDGE
      TE-COW-YES-KE
      TOM SILK

206. ADAM CATCHEM
     NANCY CATCHEM
     WILLIAM CATCHEM
     JAMES CATCHEM
     NELSON CATCHEM
     MARGARET CATCHEM
     PACE CATCHEM

207. POLLY WATERS
     AR-CHE-NUR-STUR YOUNG DUCK
     SALLY YOUNG DUCK
     LUCY WATERS

208. OO-WA-HEW-SKE

209. TAR-CHE-CHA   JOHN PATRICK (U) #13303
     LYDIA TAR-CHE-CHA   WILLIAM & MARY PATRICK (GU-GA) #13717
     AL-STAW-TAH TAR-CHE-CHA
     JIMMY TAR-CHE-CHA
     SWIMMER

210. OO-WOR-CHA-KE-SKE

211. KATY KNIGHT
     WATLEY OR BETSEY
     SAMUEL KNIGHT
     WILLIAM KNIGHT

212. NANCY GRAVES

213. KING FISHER

214. OOL-SCUN-CH-OO-WAS-KIL-KA
     QUAL-KI-OO-WAS-KIL-KA

215. MAN STANDING

216. AHEY STEALER
     MARIA STEALER
     CAH-OWE-HE STEALER

217. NANCY FAWLIN
     CHE-NOH-YUH-KI
     DARKY FAWLIN
     ETE-CAR-CAR

218. CAR-WE-LE

219. RICHARD BENGE — MARY MC CONNELL (M) #8996
BETSEY BENGE — MARY ELLIS (GM) #11649
FILD BENGE — LUCINDA B. DUNCAN (GM-GGF-GGM) #8289
ANNA BENGE — JAMES SCACEWATER (GM) #11883
DUTCH BENGE — LUCINDA FIELDS (GF) #17015
FOX BENGE — ROSS SCACEWATER (GM) #17103
LUCINDA BENGE
LIZA BENGE
THOMAS GRAFFIN

220. CATY TE-CAH-NA-KE

221. GROUND-HOG OR J. C. TROT

222. DIRT SELLER

223. MARY GANN — CATHERINE STEWART (A) #8300
GEORGE GANN — REBECCA E. CREECH (M) #929
JAMES STARR
RUTH GANN

224. BUFFALO
RACHEL BUFFALO

225. JOHN EAVEN — KATE BOLAND (F-M-B) #10733
ELIZA EAVEN
LOONEY EVAN

226. LEWIS GRIFFIN

227. HOMONY SMITH
AKEY SMITH
TE-CHAR-KE-SAH SMITH

228. NAKE-CHOC-TAW-KILLER
CHE-LAU-NUR-CHER
CHICK-KE-YAH
SALLY CHOCTAW-KILLER

229. KEE-KE

230.   RICHARD BROWN
       JIMMY BROWN
       NANCY BROWN
       WILLIAM BROWN
       NELSON BROWN
       ELLICK BROWN
       CATY BROWN
       CHER-CAW-NER

231.   CHARLES STOFLE
       NELLY STOFLE
       NANCY
       JOHN BENGE

232.   ARCH WOLF

233.   CHARLES BENGE

234.   JAMES HAMMER   KATIE CANNON (M-F) #804
       BELLOWING HAMMER
       CHU-WA-NOS-KE

235.   THOMAS BREWER
       POLLY BREWER
       ANNIE TINER

236.   GEORGE JUSTICE

237.   WAGGAN
       NANCY WAGGAN
       TAKE
       JAMES WAGGAN
       AKE WAGGAN

238.   LUCY DEW   JESSE SIXKILLER (GM) #2228
       SUSANNAH DEW
       WATTEE
       CUL-LOR-YOR-HEE DEW
       HOG-SHOTTER DEW

239.   BEN TAPPAN

240.   BEAVER TAIL

241.   ELOW-E   ELSIE WELCH (F) #3003
                                   AARON H. BUTLER (F) #3004

"ONLY THE NAMES REMAIN"
CANADIAN, DISPUTED & ILLINOIS DISTRICTS
VOLUME 2

242. JOSEPH STARR

243. SAMUEL STARR

244. PIGEON
SPEAKER
SCAR-TLE-LAUS-KE

245. CALEB STARR

246. TE-A-STAE-SKY

247. JOHN TEA-CUP
NANCY TEA-CUP
NELLY CRYING-WOLF

248. HARRY VANN
DARKEY VANN
BEAR BROWN
DRY-FOREHEAD VANN
SO-QUARE-YER VANN
CHARLOTTE VANN

249. JOSEPH RATLEY

250. CAT FIELDS   NANCY RAPER (F) #2749
LYDIA FIELDS
AHR-WE-NE-SKA FIELDS
BUCK FIELDS

251. QUATY THORNTON   WALLACE THORNTON (M) #1962

252. CHU-TAH-LAH-TAH WATTS

253. CO-TE-QUAS-KEE FIELDS

254. WILLIAM HICKS

255. HESTER FIELDS
FENCE MISSER FIELDS
AGA

256. CATY OSMON   SOPHIE KING (M-S) #1608
MARTHA OSMON
LUCINDA OSMON
ELIZABETH OSMON
VIRA OSMON

257.   ANNIE CUMMINGS

ELIZA JANE SIMS (M) #9372
WILLIAM MAHER (GM) #6910
THOMAS HARRIS (M) #7505
DORA BECK (GM) #5759
MOSES J. RATLEY (M) #5761
JOHN R. HARRIS (M) #5762

258.   EVELINE ELDERS*
JOHN LINDA*

A.K.A. NANCY E. HICKS (B) #4234
(S) #4237

259.   MINERVA RATLEY
LUCY RATLEY

JOHN RUNELS (M) #4236

260.   DELILAH MC CLEAN
CALVIN MC CLEAN
AUSTIN MC CLEAN
NANCY MC CLEAN*
JOHN MC LEAN
JOSEPH MC CLEAN *
LEWIS MC CLEAN
WILLIAM MC CLEAN*
LETITIA MC CLEAN*

NANNIE DEAN (F) #11490
MARY FRYAR (F) #11495
JESSE MC LAIN (GM) #11663
A.K.A. NANCY MORROW (M-B-S) #6591
HENRIETTA JACKSON (M) #11685
A.K.A. JOSEPH MC LAIN #15597
EDWARD MC LAIN (F) #11660
A.KA. WILLIAM MC LAIN #4054
A.K.A. MARY E. SCOTT #11226
LUNA MC CLAIN (F) #185
JESSE MC LAIN (F) #5669
SUSIE HENDRICKS (GF) #24996

261.   WILLIAM PATRICK

JOHN PATRICK (F) #13303
WILLIAM & MARY PATRICK (GF) #13713
ELLEN LILLARD (F) #15993
SUSIE KING (GF) #24043

262.   SAMUEL M. TAYLOR
AMERICA TAYLOR
CHARLOTTE MARTIN

263.   JOHN BREWER
ELIZABETH BREWER
O. H. P. BREWER
G. W. BREWER
T. F. BREWER
W. S. BREWER*
R. B. BREWER
ELIZA A. BREWER

OLIVER BREWER (F) #10782
MARTHA BENGE (F-GM-GF-A-U) #3044
LUCY SMITH (GF) #12835
CHERRIE B. JACKSON (F) #12727
W. P. BREWER (F) #12677
#5671
NANCY C. B. CASH (F) #5043
GEORGE W. BREWER (F) #12678
NANNIE E. B. RILEY (F) #12682
JOHN W. BREWER (F) #5233

264. CHARLES TIMBERLAKE   WILLIAM TIMBERLAKE (A-U) #15603
      LIZZY TIMBERLAKE
      PEGGY TIMBERLAKE
      BETSEY TIMBERLAKE

265. SUSAN TIMBERLAKE

266. ANNA RONALD
      CISCE RONALD*   A.K.A. SAN FRANCISCO MC LAUGHLIN #6791

267. SUSAN SMITH
      JACK SPEARS

268. JANE MC GILL

269. DAVID R. GOARD

270. CHARLES TAYLOR

271. CEILY

272. MARY ROSS

273. DARKA

274. FANNY BEAN   SOPHRONIA SHUGART (GM) #12847
      JEFFERSON BEAN   NANNIE FOREMAN (F-GM) #4238
      SOPHRONIA BEAN   WILLIAM HARLIN (M-GM) #4239
      RUSSEL BEAN   JAMES COBB (M) #4240
      LOUISA BEAN   ELLEN BEAN FOREMAN (F-GM) #4243
      ROBERT BEAN   RUSSELL BEAN (F-GM) #4245
      JOHN, MARY ELLEN &
      JEFFERSON BEAN (F) #8130
      WALTER S. BEAN (F) #8131
      SALLIE E. THOMPSON (F) #8132
      SALLIE LANGLEY (M) #4241
      ELLEN YATES (M) #4242
      JEFFERSON COBB (M) #4244

275. JANE WOODWARD   MARY ADAMS (GM) #13437
      ELIZABETH WOODWARD   FLORENCE LAMM (GM) #16359
      WILLIAM WOODWARD
      SARAH WOODWARD

276. JOHN WEST   KIAMINTIA C. MC CULLOUGH (M-GM-GF) #762
      RUTH WEST*   A.K.A. RUTH E. FINLEY #9153
      WILLIAM WEST   JOHN C. WEST (F) #7987
      GEORGE WEST   MARTHA CASE (F) #5238
      MARTHA WEST   JEFF & JOHN WEST (F) #5870
      JOHN WEST, JR.
      RICHARD WEST
      KI-A-MUSH-A WEST
      RUTH WEST, JR.

277. RACHEL HAMMONS
      JAMES HAMMONS
      LOUISA HAMMONS*   A.KA. LOUISA M. CAPPS (M) #9610
      ROBERT BEAR
      WOLF
      WILLIAM

278. JANE SMITH
      DAVID MILLER

279. NANCY TAYLOR*   A.K.A. NANCY J. F. WHITE #623

280. ARCH TIMBERLAKE   JESSIE E. STARNES (F) #13415
                                   JOHN STARNES (F) #11869

281. MARY ANN STARNS   FLOYD & CHARLES CANTRELL (GGM) #23254
      JEFFERSON STARNS   JEFF CREECH (GM) #759
      NANCY IVY   LILLIE W. LINT (M) #1206

282. MARGARET MERRAL*   A.K.A. MARGARET BRACKETT #401

283. THOMAS CORDREY   GIBSON ALBERTY (GGGF) #2123
      SALLY CORDREY   JOHN HAMPTON (U) #13943
      MELISSY CORDREY   MABEL BARNETT (GM-GGF) #4947
      DAVID CORDREY   JENNIE FLETCHER (GGGF) #9367
      EARLY CORDREY
      A. C. CORDREY
      CHARLOTTE I. CORDREY

284. JOHN VICKARY   SUSIE LOWERY (F) #12533

285. RACHEL

286.   ALSEY HARSKEN   SYLVESTER BOND (GM) #5841
       ANNIE HARSKEN
       JULIA HARSKEN
       ARSENE MC INTOSH
       SUSANNAH MC INTOSH

287.   D. I. FRAZIER
       MARY E. FRAZIER
       SARENE FRAZIER
       R. JANE FRAZIER
       FRANCIS FRAZIER
       ABRAHAM FRAZIER

288.   ELIZA JANE DELANE
       EMILY LEE*   A.K.A. EMILY L. CLARK (M) #2121
       MARY E. DELANE

289.   CHARLES BUSHYHEAD   MARY BARTON (GU) #141

290.   SUSANNAH FIELDS   SIRRISIA I. ROGERS (F) #4106
       RACHEL FIELDS   MARY HOOD (F) #11574
       MARY ROGERS*   #9191
       JAMES FIELDS   SUSIE FIELDS (GF) #11573
       TIM FIELDS   FRED BRINAGE (M) #22702
                              JAMES W. VANN (M) #12384

291.   A. WATTS
       CO-LE-CHE WATTS

292.   STA-HI-AH

293.   NAKA BALEW

294.   NANCY OOL-STIL-LY
       ROBERT
       SLIDE MARTIN

295.   AH-CHE-KER-SKE

296.   HANNAH ARCHILLA SMITH

297.   DIRT THROWER
       SUSANNAH
       TUN-A-TEE
       BUZZARD
       JUDGE

298.	SALLY DEER-SKIN	CHARLIE STARR (GF) #10691
	GEORGE DEER SKIN*	A.K.A. GEORGE DEERSKIN OR WATERS #895
	E-CHAR-KE	WILLIAM STARR (GF) #10693
299.	HENRY BREATH	
300.	ARCH E. GEORGE	
301.	OO-LOR-CHE-TAH	
302.	STINKING TOBACCO	
303.	NED	WA-LA-NE-TAH SCOTT (GF) #13395
304.	CAR-NUR-TE	
	SU-SAR-NIE	
305.	MARY ANN CADLE*	A.K.A. ABBIE KING #1975
306.	CHU-WA-NO-AS-KE	JAMES FOSTER (GU) #10711

END OF ILLINOIS DISTRICT

CANADIAN, ILLINOIS & DISPUTED DISTRICT INDEX:

CANADIAN, ILLINOIS & DISPUTED DISTRICT INDEX:

CANADIAN, ILLINOIS & DISPUTED DISTRICT INDEX:

CANADIAN, ILLINOIS & DISPUTED DISTRICT INDEX:

CANADIAN, ILLINOIS & DISPUTED DISTRICT INDEX:

CANADIAN, ILLINOIS & DISPUTED DISTRICT INDEX:

CANADIAN, ILLINOIS & DISPUTED DISTRICT INDEX:

HAMPTON, SANDERS 15
HAMPTON, SILAS 15
HAMPTON, SUSAN 15
HANAN, MARGARET 18
HANNON, JENNIE 18
HARLIN, ELIZABETH 13
HARLIN, JAMES 13
HARLIN, JOHN 13
HARLIN, MARY 13
HARLIN, WILLIAM 43
HARMON, NANCY 35
HARPELLY 28
HARRIS, CATY 6
HARRIS, ELIJAH 6
HARRIS, GEORGE (MORIS) 4
HARRIS, HANNAH 6
HARRIS, I-YOO-QUE 6
HARRIS, JOHN R. 42
HARRIS, MOSES 6
HARRIS, NANCY 6
HARRIS, THOMAS 42
HARRISON, NANNIE D. 11
HARSKEN, ALSEY 45
HARSKEN, ANNIE 45
HARSKEN, JULIA 45
HART, SARAH 34
HASTINGS, CATHARINE 34
HASTINGS, LOUISA J. 10
HASTINGS, NANCY 34
HAWK 32
HEAD, WALK DEER 20
HEAVY 37
HE-HA-CHEE 28
HEINRICKS, HENRY 18
HENDRICKS, SUSIE 42
HENDRIX, DAVID 13
HENRY 21
HENSLEY, HOUSTON 25
HENSLEY, JIM 25
HENSLEY, JOE 25
HENSLEY, SAMUEL 25
HERBERGER, POLLY 36
HEREFORD, SOPHRONIA 11
HETTY 20
HICKEY, BEVERLY 8
HICKEY, HENRY 8
HICKEY, MARGARET 8
HICKEY, MARY 8
HICKEY, RACHEL 8
HICKEY, THOMAS PRESTON 8
HICKS, CRAWLER 24
HICKS, JINNY 24
HICKS, NANCY E. 30, 42
HICKS, SALLY 24
HICKS, WILLIAM 41
HIGHTMAN, HENRY 16
HIGHSMITH, MARY F. 9
HILDEBRAND, JANE 18
HILDEBRAND, JOHN 10

HILDEBRAND, JOSEPH 19
HILDEBRAND, LEANDE 25
HOG, GROUND 39
HOG, TAR-KE 5
HOLLAND, LYDIA 16
HOLMES, ALSEY 34
HOLMES, DAVID 34
HOLMES, JAMES 34
HOLMES, MARY 34
HOLMES, SIMON 34
HOLMES, SUSAN 34
HOLMES, WILLIAM 35
HOOD, MARY 45
HOWELL, MARY I. 15
HOXY (NOXY) 7
HOYT, ESTHER 12
HOYT, HYNMAN 12
HOYT, LUCY 12
HOYT, LYDIA 12
HOYT, MILO 12
HOYT, SARAH 12
HOYT, SUE 12
HUBBARD, DANIEL 12
HUBBARD, JOHN 13
HUBBARD, MOSES 12
HUBBARD, THOMAS 12, 13
HUBBARD, WILKERSON 13
HUMMING-BIRD 31
HUMPHREYS, CREASY 10
HUMPHREYS, JOHN 10
HUMPHREYS, WILLIAM 10
HUNGRY, DAVID 5
HUNGRY, HENRY 5
HUNTER 25
HYETT, ANNIE 15

I:
INMAN 19
IRVING, JOE 19
ISBELL, JENNIE 17
ISBELL, MORRIS 17
ISBELL, OLIVE 17
ISBELL, THOMAS 17
IVY, NANCY 44
I-YOO-QUE-HARRIS 6
I-YOR-KA 29
I-YOR-KEE 20

J:
JACK 23
JACKSON, CHERRIE B. 42
JACKSON, HENRIETTA 42
JAMES 25, 28
JANE 14, 20, 26
JENKINS, IDA 18
JESSE 22
JINNY 33, 35
JOHN 18, 36
JOHNSON 30, 37

54

CANADIAN, ILLINOIS & DISPUTED DISTRICT INDEX:

CANADIAN, ILLINOIS & DISPUTED DISTRICT INDEX:

CANADIAN, ILLINOIS & DISPUTED DISTRICT INDEX:

CANADIAN, ILLINOIS & DISPUTED DISTRICT INDEX:

58

59

CANADIAN, ILLINOIS & DISPUTED DISTRICT INDEX:

CANADIAN, ILLINOIS & DISPUTED DISTRICT INDEX:

CANADIAN, ILLINOIS & DISPUTED DISTRICT INDEX:

62

62

CANADIAN, ILLINOIS & DISPUTED DISTRICT INDEX:

WOODWARD, JANE 43
WOODWARD, JOHN 6
WOODWARD, LEECH 26
WOODWARD, MARTHA 6
WOODWARD, SARAH 43
WOODWARD, SE-WE 26
WOODWARD, WILLIAM 43
WOOL 24
WUT-TE 4, 5
WUTTY 31

X:

Y:
YA-HO-LA 35
YATES, ELLEN 43
YEATH-CHE 32
YER-WE-LOR-SE 33
YORK-SE 35
YOUNG-BIRD 24
YOUNG, DICK 32
YOUNG DUCK, AR-CHE-NUR-STUR 38
YOUNG DUCK, SALLY 38
YOUNG-MAN 32
YOUNG PUPPY 21
YOUNG WOLF 21
YOW-NUR-OO-NUR-WOR 37

Z:

www.ingramcontent.com/pod-product-compliance
Lightning Source LLC
Chambersburg PA
CBHW081156090426
42736CB00017B/3353